WHY **YOU** ARE STILL **BROKE!**

"Change Your Thinking, Change Your Money Story"

By

Robert E. Hammond

DISCLAIMER

The information contained in this book is for informational and educational purposes only and should not be construed as financial advice. The author and publisher are not financial advisors and cannot guarantee the outcome of any financial decisions you make. Every individual's financial situation is unique, and you should consult with a qualified financial professional before making any investment decisions. While the authors have made every effort to ensure the accuracy of the information in this book, we take no responsibility for any errors or omissions.

Copyright Page

© Robert E. Hammond 2024

All rights reserved. No part of this book may be reproduced, stored in a retrieval system, or transmitted in any form or by any means – electronic, mechanical, photocopying, recording, scanning, or otherwise – without the prior written permission of the copyright holder.

WHY YOU ARE STILL BROKE!

DISCLAIMER	**2**
COPYRIGHT PAGE	**2**
PREFACE	**6**
CHAPTER 1: WHY YOU'RE STUCK IN THE BROKE ZONE	**9**
THE HIDDEN COSTS OF THE SCARCITY MINDSET	11
IDENTIFYING YOUR MONEY DEMONS	13
PLANTING THE SEEDS OF ABUNDANCE	14
FROM BROKE TO ABUNDANT	16
CHAPTER 2: WHY YOU BELIEVE YOU CAN'T BE WEALTHY.	**18**
FIXED VS. GROWTH MINDSET	18
CHAPTER 3: FROM VICTIM TO VICTOR	**24**
CHAPTER 4 CRAFTING YOUR PATH TO FINANCIAL FREEDOM	**29**
CHAPTER 5: DELAYED GRATIFICATION VS. IMPULSE SPENDING FINANCIAL FREEDOM	**38**

The Temptation of Instant Gratification. 39
The Power of Delayed Gratification 40
Shifting Your Mindset: From Impulsive Spender to Savvy Saver 41
Celebrating Milestones, Not Every Small Step 44

CHAPTER 6 WHERE GRATITUDE BLOSSOMS INTO FINANCIAL PROSPERITY 46

The Scarcity Trap: A Distorted View of Reality 46
The Abundance Mindset: A World of Possibilities 48
Gratitude: The Seed of Abundance 49
Living with Abundance: Daily Habits for Financial Growth 51

CHAPTER 8: YOUR SPENDING HABITS FOR FINANCIAL FREEDOM 54

Why We Spend What We Spend 54
From Impulsive Buyer to Mindful Spender 56
It's Not About How Much You Have, But How You Live 58
Building a Sustainable Financial Future: Beyond Budgeting 60

CHAPTER 9: EXPLORING INVESTMENT STRATEGIES FOR GROWTH 63

Understanding the Risk-Return Trade-Off 63

A BUFFET OF INVESTMENT OPTIONS: CHOOSING THE RIGHT VEHICLE	64
ALIGNING WITH YOUR GOALS AND RISK TOLERANCE	67
INVESTING THROUGHOUT LIFE'S STAGES: TAILORING YOUR STRATEGY	69

CHAPTER 10: CRUSHING DEBT AND ACHIEVING FINANCIAL FREEDOM — 72

UNDERSTANDING THE DEBT LANDSCAPE: FRIEND OR FOE?	72
DEVELOPING A DEBT-SLAYING STRATEGY	74
LIFE AFTER DEBT: BUILDING A FORTRESS OF FINANCIAL FREEDOM	78

CHAPTER 11: UNDERSTANDING INVESTMENT ACCOUNTS AND STRATEGIES — 81

CHOOSING THE RIGHT TOOLS FOR THE JOB: INVESTMENT STRATEGIES TAILORED TO ACCOUNT TYPES	84
BUILDING A STRONG FOUNDATION: ASSET ALLOCATION AND REBALANCING	86

CONCLUSION — 88

PREFACE

Let's face it, you're broke. Maybe you haven't gotten that official eviction notice yet (although the late fees are piling up), but that sinking feeling in your gut tells you something's gotta change. You hustle, you work hard, but that paycheck seems to disappear faster than a magician's rabbit.

I get it. Been there, done that. For years, I was the guy living paycheck to paycheck, ramen noodles my best friend, and my bank account a perpetual mystery. But here's the secret nobody tells you: **it wasn't my income that was the problem, it was my thinking.**

It dawned on me: the story I was telling myself about money was a total lie! A story of scarcity, limitations, and the unwavering belief that wealth was reserved for the "lucky" few.

But guess what? That story is a crock.

As an investor, I learned a fundamental truth: wealth creation isn't about blind luck or some preordained destiny. It's about **mindset**. It's about rewiring your brain to see opportunity, cultivate abundance, and make smart choices with the resources you have.

This book isn't about shaming you or blaming your circumstances. We've all been there. This is a **battle cry**, a call to arms for anyone tired of the broken cycle. Here, we'll expose the hidden beliefs keeping you stuck, and most importantly, we'll equip you with the tools and strategies to **change your story**.

Because let me tell you, you are capable of so much more than you think.

We'll be diving deep into the psychology of money, exploring the limiting beliefs that hold you back, and developing a growth mindset built for financial success. We'll talk about practical strategies like budgeting, managing debt, and even creating multiple income streams (because let's face it, one job just ain't cutting it anymore).

This book isn't about pointing fingers or shaming you for that empty bank account. It's a wake-up call, a manifesto for change. We'll crack open the skull of the "broke mindset" and expose the limiting beliefs holding you back. We'll dismantle the myths that wealth is reserved for the privileged few, and unveil the truth: financial freedom is within your grasp.

But here's the deal: it takes work. It takes a willingness to confront your money demons and rewrite your financial story. I'm not promising a get-rich-quick scheme. But I am offering a transformative roadmap, a set of tools forged in the fires of my financial journey.

This book is your investment in yourself. Consider it a down payment on a future where money anxieties fade, replaced by the freedom to pursue your dreams. Ready to become the architect of your financial future? Let's get started.

CHAPTER 1:
WHY YOU'RE STUCK IN THE BROKE ZONE

Ever feel like you're on a hamster wheel, running as fast as you can, but never getting anywhere financially? You're not alone. Millions of people are trapped in the "broke zone," a land of constant struggle and dwindling bank accounts.

But here's the thing: it doesn't have to be this way. There's a hidden culprit behind your financial woes, and it's not your income (although we'll get to that later). It's your **mindset**.

Think of your mind as a garden. If you constantly plant seeds of doubt, fear, and scarcity, what kind of harvest do you expect? A garden overflowing with financial abundance? Not likely.

The truth is, that most broke folks are operating with a scarcity mindset. This sneaky little belief whispers things like:

- "There's never enough money."

- "The rich get richer, and the poor get poorer."
- "I can't afford that."

These negative thoughts become self-fulfilling prophecies. You avoid opportunities because you believe you can't succeed, and voila, you don't.

Let me tell you a story. Back in my broke days, every penny felt precious. I'd avoid buying coffee, skip vacations, and clip coupons like a pro. But guess what? This constant focus on scarcity **attracted more scarcity** into my life.

Then, I had a revelation. What if I flipped the script? What if I started nurturing a garden of abundance?

So, I began planting new seeds. I focused on gratitude for what I did have. I visualized financial success. I actively sought out opportunities to increase my income. It wasn't easy, but slowly, my mindset began to shift.

Here's the key difference between a scarcity and abundance mindset:

- **Scarcity:** Focuses on lack, limitation, and fear.

- **Abundance:** Focuses on opportunity, growth, and possibility.

The good news? You can change your mindset. In this chapter, we'll explore:
- **The hidden costs of the scarcity mindset.**
- **How to identify limiting beliefs about money.**
- **Planting the seeds of abundance in your financial garden.**
- **Real-life examples of people who shifted their mindsets to achieve wealth.**

By the end of this chapter, you'll be ready to ditch the broke mentality and start cultivating a mindset that attracts financial abundance. Are you ready to transform your financial landscape?

The Hidden Costs of the Scarcity Mindset

The scarcity mindset might seem harmless on the surface, but it has a profound impact on your financial decisions and overall well-being. Here are some of the hidden costs:

The scarcity mindset acts like a constant voice whispering doubt, holding you back from reaching your financial potential. It tells you "You can't afford it," causing you to miss out on investments, educational opportunities, or even starting a side hustle that could bring greater wealth. This fear of running out of money can lead to impulsive spending decisions or clinging to unfulfilling jobs that offer a false sense of security over opportunities for growth. The constant worry creates a cycle of negative emotions like stress, anxiety, and even depression, hindering your ability to think clearly and make sound financial choices. Ultimately, the scarcity mindset keeps you stuck in a limited way of thinking, focused solely on "just getting by" and preventing you from dreaming big and believing in the possibility of achieving true financial security.

Here's an exercise to see if the scarcity mindset is controlling your finances:

- *Track your spending for a week. Be honest about where your money goes.*
- *Identify areas where scarcity might be influencing your choices. Do you avoid buying healthy food*

> because it's more expensive? Do you skip networking events because of the cost of a coffee?
> - **Challenge your limiting beliefs.** Ask yourself, "Is this belief truly serving me?"

Remember, scarcity is a story you tell yourself. You have the power to rewrite the narrative.

Identifying Your Money Demons

Now, let's get personal. Those limiting beliefs about money? It's time to drag them out of the shadows and confront them head-on.

Here are some common money demons that plague the broke mindset:

"I'm not good with money." This belief is often passed down through generations. Challenge it by learning about personal finance and developing a budget.

"The rich get richer, and the poor get poorer." This simply isn't true. Many wealthy individuals come from modest backgrounds. Focus on creating your path to success.

"Money is the root of all evil." Money is a tool. It can be used for good or bad. Focus on using your money to create a positive impact on your life and the lives of others.

Here's a tip: *Write down your limiting beliefs about money. Then, next to each one, write down a positive counter-belief. For example, if your limiting belief is "I'm not good with money," your counter-belief could be "I am capable of learning and becoming financially savvy."*

By identifying and challenging these limiting beliefs, you'll be well on your way to cultivating an abundance mindset.

Stay tuned for the next section, where we'll explore how to plant the seeds of abundance in your financial garden!

Planting the Seeds of Abundance

So, you've identified the weeds of scarcity choking your financial growth. Now it's time to cultivate a garden overflowing with abundance! Here are some powerful seeds you can plant:

- **Gratitude:** Shift your focus from what you lack to what you already have. Start a gratitude journal and write down three things you're grateful for each day. This simple practice trains your brain to focus on the positive aspects of your life, including your finances.
- **Visualization:** Close your eyes and picture yourself achieving your financial goals. Imagine yourself living comfortably, debt-free, and pursuing your dreams. This powerful technique helps to program your subconscious mind for success.
- **Positive Affirmations:** Repeat positive affirmations about money and abundance daily. Examples include "I am worthy of financial success," "Money flows to me easily and effortlessly," or "I am a wealth magnet." Over time, these affirmations can rewire your limiting beliefs.
- **Focus on Abundance:** Instead of constantly worrying about running out of money, focus on ways to increase your income. Explore side hustles, invest in skills development, or negotiate a raise at

your current job. Abundance thinking is about actively creating opportunities for financial growth.
- **Giving Back:** Helping others is a powerful way to cultivate abundance in your own life. Volunteer your time, donate to a worthy cause, or simply pay for someone's coffee in line. Giving fosters a sense of gratitude and opens you up to receiving abundance in return.

Remember, these seeds won't sprout overnight. Cultivating an abundance mindset takes consistent effort and positive reinforcement. But the more you nurture these seeds, the more they'll flourish in your financial garden.

From Broke to Abundant

Inspiration is key. Let's take a look at a few real-life examples of people who transformed their financial situation by shifting their mindset:

- **Sarah, the Single Mom:** After a divorce left her with mounting bills and a single income, Sarah decided to change her story. She adopted a gratitude practice, started a side hustle selling crafts online, and visualized her financial freedom. Within a year, she paid off her debt and saved enough for a down payment on a house.

- **David, the Debt-Ridden Entrepreneur:** David's business dreams were crushed by a mountain of credit card debt. He replaced his scarcity mindset with one focused on abundance. David enrolled in a financial literacy course, negotiated lower interest rates, and started a blog to share his financial journey. Today, he's debt-free and his blog helps others achieve financial freedom.

These stories are a testament to the power of changing your mindset. **You too can transform your financial reality.**

CHAPTER 2:
WHY YOU BELIEVE YOU CAN'T BE WEALTHY.

Fixed vs. Growth Mindset

Imagine that nagging voice in your head, the one that whispers doubts about your financial future. It might say things like, "Investing is just for the rich," or "I'll never be good at managing money." This, my friend, is the fixed mindset in action. It operates on the belief that your financial intelligence and earning potential are set in stone, leaving you feeling powerless to change your circumstances.

The fixed mindset acts like a mental roadblock, keeping you stuck and preventing you from achieving financial success. Remember that feeling of despair in school when you were convinced you were "bad at math" no matter how hard you tried? The fixed mindset operates similarly with finances, whispering insidious lies that hold you back.

Here's the key to breaking free: **your financial future is not predetermined**. Enter the growth mindset, a powerful belief system that acknowledges your financial skills and knowledge can be developed through effort and learning. Think of it like this: the fixed mindset keeps you stuck on a rickety old bicycle, while the growth mindset empowers you to navigate any financial terrain on a sleek, high-performance bike.

The fixed mindset can manifest in various ways, acting as a constant barrier to wealth creation. For instance, you might encounter the belief, "Investing is too complicated for me." This fixed mindset view prevents you from exploring potentially lucrative investment opportunities. It's like putting up a mental "Do Not Enter" sign before you even begin to understand the possibilities. The growth mindset, on the other hand, encourages you to seek out resources and education. It acknowledges that there's a learning curve, but it empowers you to overcome that hurdle.

Another common example is the defeatist attitude fueled by the fixed mindset: "I'll never make enough money to pay off this debt." This kind of thinking prevents you from creating a clear plan to tackle your debt. It keeps you paralyzed by the size of the problem, offering no path forward. The growth mindset, however, acknowledges the challenge but focuses on solutions. It empowers you to explore options like debt consolidation, budgeting strategies, or increasing your income. It's about taking an active approach and believing you can overcome the obstacle.

Similarly, the fixed mindset might make you believe, "Budgeting is too restrictive." This perception prevents you from taking control of your finances and making smart spending choices. It paints budgeting as a punishment, something that takes away your freedom. The growth mindset, however, recognizes budgeting as a powerful tool for achieving financial freedom. It allows you to make conscious decisions about your money and frees you from the anxiety of overspending. It's not about feeling deprived, but about making choices that align with your long-term goals.

The good news is, you can cultivate a growth mindset and unlock your financial potential. Here's how:

Embrace the learning journey. You don't need to be a financial expert overnight. Commit to ongoing learning by reading books, listening to podcasts, or taking financial literacy courses. The growth mindset celebrates the journey of acquiring knowledge and skills. Every step you take towards understanding personal finance is a victory.

Celebrate small wins. Every step towards your financial goals, big or small, deserves recognition. Acknowledge your progress, no matter how seemingly insignificant. This reinforces the growth mindset by highlighting your capabilities and motivating you to keep moving forward. Did you stick to your grocery budget this week? Did you finally pay down an extra $100 on your credit card? Celebrate these victories! They are stepping stones on your path to financial success.

Reframe your thinking about challenges. Setbacks are inevitable on the road to financial freedom. The fixed mindset sees them as failures, proof that you're not good with money. The growth mindset views them as opportunities to learn and adjust your strategies. When faced with an obstacle, ask yourself, "What can I learn from this? How can I use this experience to improve?" Did you overspend on impulse this month? Don't beat yourself up. Analyze what triggered it, and develop a plan to avoid the same mistake next time.

Surround yourself with positive influences. The company you keep matters. Connect with people who share your financial goals and can support your growth. Being around others who believe in your ability to succeed fosters a growth mindset environment. Look for online communities, local finance groups, or even a supportive friend who's also working towards financial goals. Sharing your journey with others can provide encouragement, accountability, and valuable insights.

By adopting a growth mindset, you can break free from the limitations of the fixed mindset and unlock your true financial potential. In the next chapter, we'll tackle another roadblock to financial success - the victim mentality. We'll discuss how to take ownership of your finances and empower yourself to create wealth.

CHAPTER 3:
FROM VICTIM TO VICTOR

Have you ever felt like the world is rigged against your financial success? Maybe you find yourself blaming your upbringing, your job, or even the economy for your current situation. If so, you might be clinging to the victim mentality, a dangerous mindset that keeps you stuck in a cycle of powerlessness.

This chapter dives deep into the victim mentality and equips you with the tools to transform yourself from a passive observer to an empowered victor in your financial journey.

The victim mentality whispers insidious messages in your ear. It tells you things like, "The system is rigged," or "I just don't have the same opportunities as others." While external factors can certainly influence your circumstances, this mindset prevents you from taking ownership of your financial future. It paints you as a passive observer, at the mercy of forces beyond your control.

Clinging to the victim mentality has several detrimental consequences. It reduces your sense of agency, leading to inaction and missed opportunities. It fosters increased negativity, filling your life with resentment, frustration, and a general sense of hopelessness. Perhaps most damaging, it erodes your self-esteem. Feeling like a victim undermines your sense of control and self-worth, hindering your ability to make positive financial decisions.

Here's the truth that can set you free: you have more power than you think. Shifting from victim to victor requires a fundamental change in perspective. Instead of blaming others, you take responsibility for your financial situation. This doesn't mean ignoring challenges, but rather acknowledging them and then taking proactive steps to overcome them.

The escape route from the victim mentality is paved with self-awareness and action. The first step is to identify your victim narratives. Pay attention to the stories you tell yourself about money. Are you constantly complaining about low wages or rising costs? Challenge these narratives. Focus on what you can control – your spending habits, your earning potential, and your financial education.

Embrace responsibility. Stop blaming external factors for your financial struggles. Acknowledge the role you've played in your current situation and commit to making changes. This doesn't mean self-flagellation, but rather owning your choices and learning from them.

Instead of dwelling on problems, shift your mindset towards finding solutions. Explore ways to increase your income, cut back on unnecessary expenses, or improve your financial literacy.

The victim mentality thrives on ignorance. The more you educate yourself about personal finance, the more confident you'll feel in managing your money. Here are some ways to boost your financial knowledge:

Become a lifelong learner: There are countless resources available on personal finance, from beginner guides to advanced investment strategies. Find materials that resonate with you and start learning.

Financial podcasts on the go: Financial podcasts offer a convenient way to learn while commuting, exercising, or doing chores. Many podcasts feature interviews with experts and cover a wide range of financial topics.

Invest in your future: Consider online or in-person courses on budgeting, investing, or other personal finance topics. Investing in your financial education is an investment in your future.

The key differences between the victim and victor mindsets lie in their core beliefs and resulting actions. The victim mentality focuses on external factors, leading to a negative attitude and a tendency to complain and take no action. The victor mentality, on the other hand, emphasizes personal responsibility, fostering a solution-oriented and positive outlook that drives initiative. Victims feel empowered to make changes, leading to higher self-esteem.

Remember, the journey from victim to victor is a process. There will be setbacks and moments of doubt. But by consistently focusing on what you can control and taking action towards your financial goals, you can break free from the victim mentality and create the financial future you deserve.

The next chapter will delve deeper into practical tools and strategies for building wealth and achieving financial freedom. We'll explore creating a budget, managing debt, and even building multiple income streams. Get ready to transform yourself from a financial victim into a powerful victor!

CHAPTER 4
CRAFTING YOUR PATH TO FINANCIAL FREEDOM

Feeling like you're perpetually broke often stems from a lack of direction. Without clear goals, it's easy to spend aimlessly, make impulsive financial decisions, and wander further away from financial security. This chapter equips you with powerful tools: goal setting and visualization. By mastering these techniques, you'll create a roadmap that propels you towards achieving financial freedom.

The Art of Goal Setting: Building a Foundation for Success

Effective financial goal setting isn't just about scribbling wishes on a piece of paper. It requires a strategic approach that provides clarity, focus, and most importantly, a path to achievement. Here's where the SMART framework comes into play:

Specific: Vague desires like "have more money" lack the power to move you forward. Transform them into specific, well-defined goals. Instead, say, "I will save $10,000 for a down payment on a used car within the next 18 months." This specificity allows you to visualize the goal and create a concrete plan for reaching it.

Measurable: How will you know you're making progress? Define clear metrics to track your journey. For your car down payment goal, consider opening a dedicated savings account and setting up automatic transfers to ensure consistent savings. Track your balance monthly, celebrating milestones like reaching $2,500 or $5,000 saved. Measurable progress keeps you motivated and provides a sense of accomplishment.

Attainable: Setting ambitious goals is admirable, but it's crucial to ensure they're achievable within your means. Consider your current income, existing debt obligations, and realistic saving potential. Saving $10,000 in 18 months might be a stretch if you're currently living paycheck to paycheck.

A more attainable goal might be $5,000 in 24 months, allowing you to adjust your budget and potentially increase your income through a side hustle. Remember, achieving smaller goals builds momentum and confidence, paving the way for setting even more ambitious targets in the future.

Relevant: Financial goals should align with your overall financial vision. Are you saving for a car down payment because you desire the freedom and flexibility it offers? Ensure your goals support your long-term aspirations and contribute to your broader financial well-being. Don't get caught up in societal pressures or keeping up with the Joneses. Focus on goals that resonate with your personal values and financial dreams.

Time-bound: Goals without deadlines lack urgency. Set a specific timeframe for achieving each milestone. For your car down payment, a deadline of 18 months creates a sense of urgency and motivates you to stay focused on your savings plan. Time-bound goals inject a healthy dose of pressure, keeping you accountable and moving forward.

Visualization: Programming Your Mind for Success

Visualization might sound like something out of a self-help infomercial, but its power for achieving goals has been scientifically validated. By vividly picturing yourself achieving your financial goals, you can program your subconscious mind for success. Here's how visualization works its magic:

Mental Rehearsal: Imagine yourself reaching your goals with all your senses engaged. For the car down payment, see yourself walking into a dealership, confidently negotiating a fair price, and driving your new car off the lot. Feel the excitement of freedom and accomplishment. The more vivid and detailed your visualization, the more powerful its impact. Regularly engaging in this mental rehearsal strengthens the neural pathways in your brain associated with success, making it more likely to happen in reality.

Motivation Booster: Visualizing success strengthens your desire to achieve your goals. The positive emotions associated with your mental rehearsal – the joy of driving your new car – fuel your motivation and keep you on track, even when faced with challenges or setbacks. Visualization acts as a mental reward system, reminding you of the satisfaction that awaits you upon reaching your goals.

Confidence Catalyst: Repeatedly visualizing success builds self-belief. As you see yourself achieving your goals in your mind's eye, you develop a sense of confidence in your ability to make them a reality. This unshakeable belief is crucial for overcoming obstacles and staying focused during difficult times. Visualization empowers you to take action and move past self-doubt that might otherwise hold you back.

Taking Action: Crafting Your Personalized Financial Roadmap

Now that you understand the importance of SMART goals and visualization, it's time to translate them into a tangible plan. Let's embark on the journey of crafting your personalized financial roadmap:

Unleash Your Financial Dreams: Start by brainstorming your long-term financial aspirations. Don't hold back!

Write down everything you desire, no matter how ambitious or seemingly out of reach it may seem. Do you dream of traveling the world first class, retiring early on a tropical beach, or starting your own business and becoming financially independent? Write freely, allowing yourself to envision a future brimming with financial freedom and fulfillment.

Break Down the Big Picture: Large, distant goals can feel overwhelming and paralyzing. To make them feel more achievable, break down your big dreams into smaller, more manageable milestones. For example, if your ultimate dream is early retirement on a tropical beach, some milestones might include:

Saving a specific amount of money per year towards retirement.

Researching and choosing a cost-effective location for retirement living.

Exploring ways to generate passive income streams to supplement your retirement savings.

Assessing your current skillset and identifying opportunities to develop skills that could lead to remote work options in retirement.

By creating these smaller, actionable steps, your once-distant dream starts to feel attainable.

Turn Dreams into SMART Goals: Now that you have your milestones identified, it's time to apply the SMART framework to each one. Let's revisit the example of saving for retirement:

Specific: Instead of a vague goal of "saving more for retirement," set a specific target like "save an additional $5,000 per year for retirement over the next five years."

Measurable: Track your progress by monitoring your retirement savings account balance regularly. Celebrate reaching milestones like $5,000 or $10,000 saved.

Attainable: Consider your current income and budget realistically. Saving an additional $5,000 per year might be achievable if you explore ways to cut back on expenses or increase your income.

Relevant: Ensure your increased retirement savings align with your long-term goal of early retirement.

Time-bound: Set a specific timeframe for achieving your milestone, such as saving an additional $5,000 per year over the next five years.

By making your goals SMART, you create a clear roadmap and hold yourself accountable for progress.

Visualize Your Success: Take time each day to vividly visualize yourself achieving your goals. For your retirement savings goal, see yourself relaxing on that beach, financially secure, and living your dream life. Feel the peace of mind and satisfaction of achieving financial freedom. The more you engage in this visualization, the more you program your subconscious mind for success.

Track, Celebrate, and Adapt: Your financial roadmap is a living document, not set in stone. Regularly track your progress towards your goals and celebrate milestones along the way. This reinforces positive financial behaviors and keeps you motivated. If your circumstances change, be adaptable and adjust your goals or milestones as needed.

Remember, financial freedom is a journey, not a destination. By setting SMART goals, engaging in visualization, and tracking your progress, you'll equip yourself with the tools to navigate the road toward financial success. Embrace the journey, celebrate your wins, and never lose sight of the amazing financial future you're building.

CHAPTER 5:
DELAYED GRATIFICATION VS. IMPULSE SPENDING FINANCIAL FREEDOM

Let's be honest, sometimes it feels like everywhere you turn, there's a pressure to spend money. That delicious coffee every morning might seem small, but those little expenses can really add up. Plus, with all the "must-have" sales and promotions blasting us from our phones, it's easy to get caught up in the moment and buy things we don't really need. These instant pick-me-ups might feel good in the short term, but they can seriously hurt your long-term financial goals.

This chapter delves into the battle between delayed gratification and impulse spending, equipping you with strategies to break the cycle of instant gratification and build healthy financial habits that pave the way for a secure and fulfilling future.

The temptation of instant gratification.

Instant gratification is the desire for immediate pleasure or reward. It's the psychological urge to satisfy your wants right now, regardless of the consequences. The problem with instant gratification is that it's often a double-edged sword. While it can provide a temporary dopamine rush, it can also lead to a cascade of negative financial repercussions:

Debt Accumulation Trap: Frequent impulse purchases can quickly snowball into credit card debt. With high interest rates compounding, every latte adds up, draining your financial resources and making it harder to save for important goals. Before you know it, you're stuck in a cycle of minimum payments, further hindering your progress.

Missed Opportunities for Growth: Money spent on impulse buys is money not saved for your future goals. Whether it's a down payment on a house, a dream vacation, or a comfortable retirement, these impulsive purchases chip away at your ability to build a secure financial future.

Breeds Poor Financial Habits: The more you indulge in impulsive spending, the more it becomes ingrained in your behavior. It creates a vicious cycle where resisting temptation becomes increasingly difficult. You become conditioned to prioritize immediate gratification over long-term financial well-being.

The Power of Delayed Gratification

Delayed gratification is the ability to resist the urge for immediate pleasure for a larger, long-term benefit. It's about making conscious choices today that will lead to a more secure and fulfilling financial future. Think of it as an investment in your future self. Here's how delayed gratification empowers you to take control of your finances:

Financial Control and Empowerment: By prioritizing your long-term goals, you gain control over your finances. You're not a puppet on the strings of every passing impulse. Delayed gratification empowers you to make conscious spending choices that align with your financial vision.

Goal Achievement: Building Your Dreams, Brick by Brick: Delayed gratification allows you to consistently save and invest for future goals. This steady accumulation of resources paves the way for financial security and achieving your dreams, whether it's owning a home, traveling the world, or retiring early.

Increased Discipline: Building the Muscles for Financial Fitness: The more you practice delaying gratification, the more disciplined you become in your spending habits. This discipline spills over into other areas of your life, creating a sense of empowerment and control. It's like building the "financial fitness muscles" you need to navigate challenges and opportunities.

Shifting Your Mindset: From Impulsive Spender to Savvy Saver

Breaking the cycle of instant gratification and embracing delayed gratification requires a conscious shift in mindset. Here are some practical strategies to reprogram your brain and become a master of the art of "no" when faced with an impulsive purchase:

Identify Your Triggers: The first step is self-awareness. What situations or emotions trigger your impulse spending? Is it boredom scrolling through social media that leads to online shopping sprees? Maybe it's stress eating that results in unhealthy takeout purchases? Once you identify your triggers, you can develop coping mechanisms to avoid falling into the trap. For example, if boredom triggers spending, replace scrolling with a walk or calling a friend.

Create a Budget and Track Your Spending: Knowledge is power. Having a clear budget helps you understand where your money goes and identify areas where you can cut back on unnecessary spending. Tracking your expenses allows you to see how your daily choices affect your long-term goals. Seeing the numbers in black and white can be a powerful motivator to change your spending behavior.

Embrace the Waiting Game: The Power of a Night's Sleep: Develop a "sleep-on-it" rule before making any major purchases. Give yourself time to consider whether it's an impulse buy or something that truly aligns with your needs and long-term goals. Often, the urge to buy impulsively will fade away overnight. Sleeping on it allows you to make a rational decision, not an emotional one fueled by instant gratification.

Focus on the Bigger Picture: Visualization – Your Secret Weapon: Whenever you're tempted by an impulsive purchase, remind yourself of your long-term financial goals. Don't just think about them – visualize them! See yourself achieving those goals, whether it's relaxing on a beach after a successful early retirement or celebrating a housewarming party in your dream home. The more vivid your visualization, the more powerful its impact. This mental rehearsal strengthens the neural pathways in your brain associated with your goals, making them seem more attainable and the impulsive purchase less appealing.

Seek Alternatives: Gratifying Your Cravings Without Breaking the Bank: If you find yourself craving instant gratification, find healthier ways to satisfy it. Maybe you're craving a shopping spree because you're feeling stressed – go for a walk-in nature or listen to calming music instead. If it's a social connection you seek, call a friend or family member for a chat. By identifying the underlying need and finding a healthy alternative, you can avoid falling prey to impulse spending.

Celebrating Milestones, Not Every Small Step

Delayed gratification doesn't mean depriving yourself forever. The key is to establish a healthy reward system. Set milestones for your savings goals and reward yourself with something you truly value once you reach them. This reinforces your positive financial behaviors and keeps you motivated on your journey toward financial freedom. For example, reaching a specific savings target for your down payment might warrant a celebratory dinner or a weekend getaway. Just remember, the reward should be meaningful and reserved for milestones, not every small step along the way.

Changing your spending habits takes time and effort. Don't be discouraged if you slip up occasionally. We all do! The important thing is to learn from your mistakes, pick yourself up, and recommit to your long-term financial goals. By prioritizing delayed gratification and making conscious spending choices, you'll be well on your way to building a secure and fulfilling future. You'll be mastering the art of "no" to impulsive spending and saying "yes" to financial freedom.

CHAPTER 6
WHERE GRATITUDE BLOSSOMS INTO FINANCIAL PROSPERITY

Feeling perpetually broke can often be traced back to a fundamental belief: there's not enough. This scarcity mindset, the idea that the world has limited resources and financial success is a zero-sum game, can be a major roadblock on your path to financial freedom. It breeds negativity, fear, and behaviours that sabotage your financial well-being. However, there's a powerful antidote: the abundance mindset. This chapter explores the connection between gratitude and abundance and equips you with practical strategies to cultivate a mindset that attracts financial prosperity.

The Scarcity Trap: A Distorted View of Reality

The scarcity mindset is like looking through a dusty, cracked window. It distorts your view of reality, making everything seem limited and out of reach. Here's how a scarcity mindset can hinder your financial progress:

Hyper-focus on Lack: People with a scarcity mindset are constantly fixated on what they don't have. Their attention is drawn to every empty bank account, every unpaid bill, and every missed opportunity. This relentless focus on lacks breeds negativity and fear, leading to behaviours that sabotage financial growth. For example, someone with a scarcity mindset might hold onto limiting beliefs about money, like "I'm not good with money" or "Rich people are greedy." These beliefs can prevent them from taking calculated risks or exploring new income streams.

Limited Possibilities: The scarcity mindset makes it difficult to see opportunities for abundance. People become stuck in a "what if I fail?" mentality, missing out on potential avenues for financial success. They might hesitate to invest in themselves through education or skill development, fearing the potential loss more than the possibility of significant gains. This narrow perspective keeps them trapped in a cycle of limited options and limited resources.

Unhealthy Competition: Those with a scarcity mindset view others' success as a threat. They believe that if someone else wins, they must lose. This fosters a competitive and stressful environment, hindering collaboration and hindering their growth. They might be hesitant to share knowledge or network with others for fear of giving away a competitive edge.

The Abundance Mindset: A World of Possibilities

The abundance mindset, on the other hand, is like having a crystal-clear window – it allows you to see the world brimming with possibilities and opportunities. Here are the benefits of cultivating an abundance mindset:

Appreciation Breeds More: When you focus on and appreciate what you already have, you shift your energy from lack to abundance. This positive energy, like a magnet, attracts more of what you desire, including financial blessings. By appreciating your current resources, your health, your skills, and your support system, you signal to the universe that you are open to receiving more.

Openness to Opportunities: The abundance mindset allows you to see possibilities for growth everywhere. You become more open to learning new skills, exploring new ventures, and taking calculated risks that can lead to financial success. Instead of fearing failure, you view it as a learning experience and a stepping stone on your path to abundance.

Collaboration for Success: Those with an abundance mindset believe there's enough for everyone. This fosters collaboration and a sense of community, which can lead to valuable partnerships and opportunities. You understand that by helping others succeed, you also increase your chances of success. You're more likely to share knowledge, network with others, and build relationships that can open doors to new ventures and financial growth.

Gratitude: The Seed of Abundance

Gratitude is the fertile ground from which the abundance mindset blossoms. By appreciating what you already have, you signal to the universe that you are open to receiving more. Here are some practices to cultivate an attitude of gratitude:

Start a Gratitude Journal: Dedicate a few minutes each day to write down things you're grateful for, big or small. It could be something as simple as a delicious meal, a beautiful sunset, or a supportive friend. Regularly reflecting on your blessings keeps you grounded, fosters a positive outlook, and reminds you of the abundance already present in your life.

Practice Daily Gratitude: Gratitude isn't just a once-a-day activity. Train yourself to take mental pauses throughout the day to appreciate simple things. Appreciate your job that provides an income, your home that offers shelter, or even the fact that you woke up this morning with the opportunity to create a financially secure future. These small moments of gratitude shift your focus from lack to abundance and cultivate a sense of wholeness.

Express Gratitude to Others: Let the people in your life know how much you appreciate them. A heartfelt thank you to a colleague, a handwritten note to a mentor, or simply expressing appreciation to your family for their love and support – these gestures strengthen relationships and reinforce the idea of abundance in your life. By expressing gratitude to others, you create a ripple effect of positivity that reinforces your sense of abundance.

Living with Abundance: Daily Habits for Financial Growth

Cultivating an abundance mindset goes beyond just feeling grateful. Here are some actionable practices you can incorporate into your daily life to attract financial prosperity:

Grateful Visualization: In your daily visualization exercises, weave in an element of gratitude. As you visualize yourself achieving your financial goals, like owning a home or travelling the world, express deep appreciation for the resources and opportunities you already have. This reinforces the idea that you are worthy of abundance and that you are on the right path to achieving your dreams.

Celebrate Milestones, Big and Small: Don't wait until you reach your ultimate financial goal to celebrate.

Acknowledge and celebrate smaller milestones along the way. Reaching a specific savings target, getting a promotion at work, or completing a skill-development course – these are all victories worth celebrating. Celebrating milestones reinforces positive financial behaviors, keeps you motivated on your journey, and reminds you of the progress you've already made.

Give Back to Cultivate Abundance: Giving back to your community, even in small ways, fosters a sense of abundance and strengthens your connection to the universe. Volunteer your time, donate to a cause you care about, or simply help someone in need. Giving attracts more giving, both financially and emotionally. When you share your resources and talents with others, you open yourself up to receiving more abundance in return. The universe has a way of rewarding those who share their blessings.

Cultivating an abundance mindset is a continuous journey, not a destination. There will be times when negativity creeps in, but don't be discouraged. Gently redirect your focus and continue practising gratitude and visualization.

By consistently nurturing an abundance mindset, you'll attract opportunities, open doors to financial prosperity, and create a life filled with abundance and fulfilment. Remember, the world is brimming with possibilities, and you are worthy of receiving your share. So go forth with an open mind, a grateful heart, and the belief that abundance awaits!

CHAPTER 8:
YOUR SPENDING HABITS FOR FINANCIAL FREEDOM

Our relationship with money is a complex dance. We dream of financial security, yet find ourselves hitting the "buy now" button a little too readily. We might meticulously craft a budget, only to discover our hard-earned cash mysteriously vanishing before the month ends. This chapter delves into the fascinating psychology behind spending and equips you with powerful strategies to master your spending habits and waltz your way n toward financial freedom.

Why We Spend What We Spend

Understanding the underlying forces that shape our spending decisions is the first step towards taking control. Here are some key psychological factors that influence our financial choices:

Emotional Eating...of Retail Therapy: We often turn to shopping as a coping mechanism for negative emotions like stress, boredom, or loneliness. The fleeting pleasure of a new purchase can provide a temporary emotional fix, but it rarely addresses the root cause of the issue. This "retail therapy" can quickly lead to financial strain and a mountain of stuff that doesn't bring lasting joy.

The Comparison Trap: Keeping Up with the Filtered Highlights Reel: social media and advertising are masters of portraying seemingly perfect lifestyles. We're constantly bombarded with images of people on exotic vacations, sporting the latest designer trends, and living in impeccably decorated homes. This relentless social comparison can fuel feelings of inadequacy and pressure us to keep up with the Joneses, leading to impulse purchases to maintain a certain appearance or status symbol. Remember, social media is a highlight reel, not a reflection of reality.

The Marketing Maven's Mind Games: Marketers are like skilled illusionists, adept at pulling on our heartstrings and exploiting our desires. They use clever tactics like scarcity marketing ("Only 5 left in stock!") and limited-time offers ("This offer ends at midnight!") to create a sense of urgency and trigger impulsive buying decisions. Don't fall prey to these marketing tricks! Take a deep breath and remind yourself that you are in control of your spending.

The Instant Gratification Gremlin: In today's fast-paced world, we crave instant gratification. The ease of online shopping with one-click purchases and readily available credit can make it tempting to buy things we don't necessarily need, simply because we want them right now. This focus on instant gratification can lead to a cycle of debt and hinder our ability to achieve long-term financial goals.

From Impulsive Buyer to Mindful Spender

By recognizing the psychological triggers behind our spending habits, we can develop strategies to make more conscious and controlled financial decisions. Here are some practical steps to transform yourself from an impulsive buyer into a mindful spender:

Unmask Your Spending Triggers: Become a detective of your financial behavior. Reflect on your spending patterns. What situations or emotions typically lead you to overspend? Do you mindlessly browse online shopping sites when stressed? Do you get swept up in the excitement of a crowded sale? Once you identify your triggers, you can develop coping mechanisms to avoid falling prey to them. For example, if stress shopping is your weakness, develop healthy stress-relieving activities like exercise, meditation, or spending time in nature.

Practice Mindful Spending: Every Penny Counts: Slow down and inject intentionality into your purchases. Ask yourself a series of questions before swiping your card or clicking "buy": Do I truly need this item, or is it just a want? Could I borrow it from a friend or find a cheaper alternative? Taking a moment to reflect and prioritize needs over wants can help you avoid unnecessary purchases and keep your hard-earned money in your pocket.

Craft a Budget and Track Your Spending: Knowledge is Power: A budget is your financial roadmap. Allocate your income towards essential expenses like housing, food, and utilities. Don't forget to factor in savings goals and a designated amount for discretionary spending. Numerous budgeting apps and tools can simplify this process. Tracking your spending allows you to identify areas where you can cut back and make adjustments to your budget as needed. Seeing your spending patterns in black and white can be a powerful motivator to take control of your finances.

Embrace Delayed Gratification: Invest in Experiences, Not Stuff: Shift your focus from the fleeting thrill of instant gratification to the long-term satisfaction of achieving your financial goals. Instead of making that impulse purchase, put the money towards your savings goals or an experience that will create lasting memories. Think about a weekend getaway with loved ones, a stimulating learning course, or volunteering for a cause you care about. Experiences often bring more joy and fulfillment than material possessions.

It's Not About How Much You Have, But How You Live

Financial freedom isn't just about accumulating a large bank account; it's about living a fulfilling life on your terms.

Here's how to cultivate a mindset that prioritizes experiences and rich living over the constant acquisition of material possessions:

Invest in Experiences that Create Lasting Memories: Prioritize experiences that bring you joy and connection with loved ones. This could be anything from a weekend getaway exploring a new city to a cooking class with friends or a concert ticket to see your favorite band. Experiences often create lasting memories that you can cherish for years to come, unlike material possessions that can depreciate or become obsolete.

Embrace Minimalism: Declutter Your Space and Simplify Your Life: Minimalism is the practice of intentionally living with only the things you truly need and value. Declutter your physical space by getting rid of unused possessions. This not only frees up physical space but also allows you to appreciate what you already have and reduces the urge to acquire more. Minimalism can also free up financial resources that can be directed towards experiences or other meaningful pursuits.

Cultivate an Attitude of Gratitude: Shift your focus from what you lack to appreciating what you already have. Practice daily gratitude by reflecting on the things you're grateful for, big or small. This could be your health, your supportive family, your cosy home, or even a delicious cup of coffee in the morning. When you focus on appreciating what you possess, you become less susceptible to the allure of acquiring more and find greater satisfaction in your current life.

Building a Sustainable Financial Future: Beyond Budgeting

Mastering your spending habits is an ongoing process that requires commitment and discipline. Here are some additional tips to build a sustainable financial future that goes beyond just budgeting:

Automate Your Finances: Set It and Forget It: Set up automatic transfers to savings and investment accounts. This ensures you're consistently saving towards your goals and removes the temptation to spend that money on impulse purchases. Automating your finances allows you to "pay yourself first" and frees up mental space to focus on other areas of your life.

Find a Side Hustle to Supplement Your Income: Consider starting a side hustle to generate additional income. This could be anything from freelance writing or online tutoring to selling crafts or baked goods online. The extra income can help you reach your financial goals faster and provide a financial cushion for unexpected expenses. Remember, a side hustle shouldn't feel like another overwhelming burden. Choose something you enjoy and that fits into your existing schedule.

Challenge Yourself Regularly: Keep Your Goals in Focus: Regularly assess your progress and challenge yourself to improve your financial habits. Set new savings goals or try a spending challenge to see how much you can save in a specific period. This keeps you motivated and engaged on your journey towards financial freedom. Remember, small, consistent improvements add up over time and can lead to significant results.

Changing your spending habits and achieving financial freedom takes time and effort. Don't be discouraged by setbacks. Everyone makes mistakes. The important thing is to learn from them, pick yourself up, and recommit to your financial goals. By applying the strategies outlined in this chapter, you can break free from the cycle of impulsive spending, take control of your finances, and build a life of abundance and fulfillment. You deserve financial freedom, and it is within your reach. Now go forth, armed with knowledge and empowered by intention, and create the rich life you desire!

CHAPTER 9:
EXPLORING INVESTMENT STRATEGIES FOR GROWTH

Investing is the rocket fuel that propels you toward financial freedom. It allows you to harness the magic of compound interest, where your money grows not only on its initial value but also on the accumulated interest over time. This chapter equips you with the knowledge to navigate the investment landscape, choose the right vehicles for your goals, and launch yourself on a prosperous journey.

Understanding the Risk-Return Trade-Off

Before embarking on your investment adventure, it's crucial to grasp the fundamental relationship between risk and return. Think of them as two sides of the same coin:

Risk: This refers to the possibility of losing some or all of your invested capital. Imagine investing in a promising new startup – the potential for high returns is enticing, but there's also a chance the company could fail, and you could lose your entire investment. Stocks are generally considered riskier than bonds, but they also offer the potential for higher returns.

Return: This refers to the profit or gain generated by your investment. It can come in two forms: capital appreciation (an increase in the value of your investment) and income generation (dividends or interest payments). For example, if you buy a stock for $100 and it increases in value to $120, you've experienced a 20% capital appreciation. If that same stock also pays out a $2 annual dividend, you're earning additional income on your investment.

A Buffet of Investment Options: Choosing the Right Vehicle

The investment world offers a diverse menu of options, each with its own unique characteristics and risk profile. Here's a closer look at some of the most popular choices:

Stocks: Owning stock makes you a part-owner of a company. When a company performs well, its stock price typically rises, offering you capital appreciation. However, stock prices can also be volatile, meaning they can fluctuate significantly in the short term. Think of them as a high-speed rollercoaster ride with the potential for thrilling gains but also the risk of stomach-churning drops.

Bonds: Consider bonds as IOUs from governments or corporations. You essentially loan them money for a set period, and in return, they pay you a fixed interest rate at regular intervals. Bonds are generally considered less risky than stocks because they offer a more predictable return. However, they typically offer lower potential returns than stocks. Imagine bonds as a comfortable train journey – you might not reach your destination as quickly, but you're more likely to arrive safely and on time.

Mutual Funds: Think of mutual funds as investment baskets. Professional fund managers pool money from multiple investors and invest it in a diversified portfolio of stocks, bonds, or other assets. This diversification helps spread out risk – if one investment performs poorly, the others can help balance it out. Mutual funds offer a convenient way to invest in a variety of assets without having to pick individual stocks or bonds yourself.

Exchange-Traded Funds (ETFs): Similar to mutual funds, ETFs hold a basket of assets. The key difference is that ETFs trade on stock exchanges throughout the day, like individual stocks. This allows for more flexibility and potentially lower fees compared to some actively managed mutual funds. Imagine ETFs as a self-service buffet where you can choose from a variety of pre-assembled investment options and potentially pay less for the convenience.

Real Estate: Investing in real estate can be a lucrative path to wealth creation, but it requires significant upfront capital. You can either buy property directly and rent it out for income, or invest in Real Estate Investment Trusts (REITs) which allow you to own a share of a portfolio of income-producing real estate. While real estate offers the potential for both rental income and property value appreciation, it also comes with ongoing management responsibilities, like repairs and tenant issues. Think of real estate as a spacious mansion with a beautiful garden – it offers ample space for growth but also requires a lot of upkeep.

Aligning with Your Goals and Risk Tolerance

The optimal investment strategy for you is like a custom-made suit – it needs to be tailored to your circumstances. Here are some key factors to consider when building your investment portfolio:

Investment Time Horizon: How long do you plan to keep your money invested before needing it? Generally, the longer your time horizon, the more risk you can tolerate. For example, if you're saving for retirement 20 years away, you can invest in stocks for potential long-term growth. However, if you're saving for a down payment on a house in 2 years, you might prioritize bonds or other less-risky investments

Investment Time Horizon: Think of your time horizon as a roadmap. A longer time horizon allows you to take the scenic route with some bumps and detours (higher-risk investments with the potential for greater returns) because you have time to recover from market fluctuations. A shorter time horizon necessitates a more direct route (lower-risk investments with more predictable returns) to ensure your money is readily available when you need it.

Financial Goals: What are you working so hard to achieve? Is it a comfortable retirement, your child's college education, or a dream vacation around the world? Your investment strategy should support your specific goals and the timeframe associated with each. For example, retirement savings might require a more conservative approach with a focus on income generation, while a college fund might have a higher allocation towards growth-oriented stocks.

Risk Tolerance: How comfortable are you with the possibility of your investments losing value? Some investors are thrill-seekers who enjoy the excitement of potentially high returns, even if it comes with a higher degree of risk. Others are more cautious and prioritize the security of their principal investment. Understanding your risk tolerance is crucial for choosing the right asset allocation for your portfolio. Imagine yourself on a rollercoaster – some people love the adrenaline rush of a daring loop-de-loop, while others prefer the gentler ride of a carousel. Choose investments that match your risk tolerance and comfort level.

Investing Throughout Life's Stages: Tailoring Your Strategy

Your investment strategy should evolve as you navigate different life stages. Here's a general roadmap for different age groups:

Young Investors (Early 20s-30s): Youth is on your side! Young investors typically have a longer time horizon and can afford to take on higher risks. They may focus on stocks and stock-based mutual funds for potential long-term growth. Think of it as planting seeds – the earlier you start investing, the more time your money has to grow.

Middle-Aged Investors (40s-50s): As you approach midlife, your risk tolerance may shift slightly as retirement draws closer. Your investment mix might incorporate a more balanced approach with a combination of stocks, bonds, and other asset classes. Imagine yourself pruning your investment garden – you might trim back on some riskier holdings and add more stable investments to ensure your portfolio is well-diversified.

Pre-Retirees and Retirees (60s+): As retirement nears, income generation and capital preservation become paramount. Your investment strategy may shift towards a more conservative allocation, with a focus on bonds, dividend-paying stocks, and other income-producing assets. Think of it as harvesting your investment crops – you want to ensure a steady stream of income to support your golden years.

Remember: Investing is a marathon, not a sprint. Develop a long-term investment plan, diversify your portfolio across different asset classes, and avoid making impulsive decisions based on market noise. Don't be afraid to seek professional financial advice to tailor an investment strategy that aligns with your unique circumstances and goals. With knowledge, discipline, and a well-diversified approach, you can build your wealth arsenal and propel yourself toward a secure and prosperous future. Now set sail on your exciting investment voyage, equipped with the knowledge and tools you need to navigate the financial seas with confidence. Remember, even the most experienced sailors encounter rough waters occasionally. Stay the course, weather the storms, and you'll be well on your way to reaching your financial destination.

CHAPTER 10:
CRUSHING DEBT AND ACHIEVING FINANCIAL FREEDOM

Debt can feel like a relentless beast, constantly draining your financial resources and hindering your aspirations. It casts a long shadow, limiting your ability to save for the future, plan for emergencies, or pursue your dreams. This chapter equips you with the knowledge and tools to slay this debt dragon, break free from its shackles, and reclaim control of your financial destiny.

Understanding the Debt Landscape: Friend or Foe?

Debt isn't inherently bad. Used strategically, it can be a powerful tool to achieve financial goals like purchasing a home or investing in your education. However, the key lies in understanding the different types of debt and their impact on your financial well-being. Here's a deeper look at the two main categories:

High-Interest Debt: The Vicious Cycle: This category encompasses credit card debt, payday loans, and some retail store financing. These debts are like hungry predators, carrying exorbitant interest rates that can quickly spiral out of control. Imagine a credit card with a 20% interest rate. If you only make the minimum payment each month, a significant portion of your payment goes towards interest, not the actual principal amount. This creates a vicious cycle where your debt seems to grow even if you're making payments! High-interest debt should be your primary target for elimination due to its significant financial burden.

Low-Interest Debt: Partnering for Progress: Mortgages and student loans often fall under this category. While still in debt, they typically have lower interest rates compared to their high-interest counterparts. Think of a student loan with a 5% interest rate – it's like a supportive partner who helps you finance your education, but at a lower cost. However, the large principal number of mortgages and student loans can still be a significant financial burden, requiring careful budgeting and a strategic repayment plan.

Developing a Debt-Slaying Strategy

There's no one-size-fits-all approach to slaying the debt monster. The most effective strategy depends on your unique financial situation, personality, and goals. Here are some popular debt repayment methods, each with its advantages:

The Debt Avalanche: A Surgical Strike: This method prioritizes paying off the debt with the highest interest rate first, regardless of the outstanding balance. Imagine wielding a laser sword, precisely targeting the most expensive debt (the one with the highest interest rate) to eliminate it quickly. By eliminating the debt that's accruing the most interest charges, you save money in the long run. This method can be particularly motivating as you see those high-interest debts disappear from your list, providing a sense of accomplishment and progress.

The Debt Snowball: Building Momentum: This method focuses on paying off the debt with the smallest balance first, regardless of the interest rate. Think of it like throwing a snowball that grows larger with each successful repayment. Paying off even a small debt completely can provide a significant psychological boost and a surge of motivation. This can be particularly helpful if you're feeling overwhelmed by a mountain of debt. Seeing quick wins with smaller debts can keep you engaged and on track for tackling the larger balances later.

Debt Consolidation: A Unified Front: This strategy involves combining multiple debts into a single loan with a lower interest rate. Imagine merging your scattered debts into a single, powerful army. Debt consolidation simplifies your repayment process by having one monthly payment instead of multiple ones. It can also potentially save you money on interest charges if you qualify for a lower interest rate on the consolidated loan. However, it's important to choose a fixed-rate loan with a shorter repayment term to avoid getting stuck in debt for even longer. Remember, consolidation doesn't eliminate your debt – it just changes the way you manage it.

Beyond the Numbers: The Mental Game of Debt Repayment

Conquering debt requires not just financial planning but also mental fortitude. Here are some strategies to fortify your mental armor and stay on track:

Identify Your "Why": Define your ultimate purpose for becoming debt-free. Is it achieving financial independence, planning a dream vacation, or leaving a legacy for your children? A clear and compelling "why" will fuel your determination during challenging times. Write down your goals and post them somewhere visible as a constant reminder of your motivation.

Track Your Progress: Visualize Your Victory: Seeing your progress is a powerful motivator. Use a budgeting app, a debt tracker spreadsheet, or even a simple whiteboard to chart your debt reduction journey. Celebrate milestones, big and small, to acknowledge your achievements. Seeing the debt numbers decrease can be incredibly motivating and keep you focused on your goal.

Embrace a "Less is More" Mentality: Reduce unnecessary spending to free up more resources for debt repayment. Challenge yourself to live on a budget and avoid taking on new debt. Look for creative ways to cut back on expenses without sacrificing your quality of life. Could you brown-bag your lunch instead of eating out? Do you have subscriptions you no longer use? Every dollar saved is a dollar that can go towards crushing your debt and achieving financial freedom. Remember, true wealth isn't about how much you own, but about being free from the burden of debt.

Seek Support: You Don't Have to Fight Alone: Don't be afraid to reach out for help and accountability. Talk to a trusted friend, family member, or financial advisor about your debt repayment goals. There's strength in numbers. Having someone to confide in and celebrate your progress with can make a world of difference. Consider joining a debt-free community online or in your local area. Sharing your struggles and successes with others who are on a similar journey can be incredibly motivating and provide valuable support.

Life After Debt: Building a Fortress of Financial Freedom

Once you've vanquished the debt monster, it's crucial to build strong defenses to prevent it from returning and to safeguard your financial freedom. Here are some key strategies to maintain your financial well-being:

Live Below Your Means: Don't Inflate Your Lifestyle: Avoid lifestyle inflation – the tendency to increase your spending as your income increases. Just because you're no longer burdened by debt payments doesn't mean you should start spending frivolously. Continue living frugally and prioritize saving and investing your money. Remember, financial freedom is about having choices, and that requires maintaining a healthy balance between your income and expenses.

Build an Emergency Fund: Your Financial Safety Net: Create a solid emergency fund to cover unexpected expenses like car repairs or medical bills. Having an emergency fund prevents you from resorting to credit cards or other forms of debt during financial setbacks. Aim to save 3-6 months of living expenses to act as a buffer during emergencies.

Automate Your Finances: Set It and Forget It: Set up automatic payments for your bills to avoid late fees and potential damage to your credit score. Automating your finances ensures your bills are paid on time and frees up mental space to focus on other areas of your life.

Monitor Your Credit Regularly: Be Vigilant: Maintain good financial hygiene by regularly monitoring your credit report for errors and fraudulent activity. Dispute any inaccuracies promptly to maintain a good credit score, which can qualify you for better loan rates in the future. Think of your credit score as a key that unlocks financial opportunities – safeguarding its accuracy is crucial.

The journey to becoming debt-free is a marathon, not a sprint. There will be setbacks and temptations along the way. The key is to stay focused on your long-term goals, celebrate your progress, and learn from any missteps. With dedication, perseverance, and the strategies outlined in this chapter, you can slay the debt dragon, achieve financial freedom, and unlock a brighter financial future. Now go forth, armed with knowledge and empowered by determination, and pave the path to financial security and peace of mind. Don't wait any longer! Empower yourself with financial knowledge and embark on your debt-free journey today. Financial freedom is within your reach!

CHAPTER 11:
UNDERSTANDING INVESTMENT ACCOUNTS AND STRATEGIES

Congratulations! You've conquered the debt monster and are ready to embark on the exciting journey of building wealth through investing. But before you jump into the stock market like a kid in a ball pit, it's crucial to understand the different investment accounts available and how they can impact your financial goals. This chapter equips you with the knowledge to choose the right investment playground – your investment accounts – and the strategies to make your money grow efficiently and effectively.

Think of investment accounts as specialized toolboxes for your investment journey. Each account type offers unique benefits and tax implications, and choosing the right one depends on the tools you need to achieve your financial goals and the timeframe you have to use them. Here's a breakdown of some common investment accounts:

Taxable Brokerage Accounts: Your All-Purpose Toolbox: These accounts are the most versatile, allowing you to invest in a wide range of assets like stocks, bonds, mutual funds, and ETFs. Imagine them as a well-stocked toolbox with all the essentials – hammers (stocks for growth), screwdrivers (bonds for stability), wrenches (mutual funds for diversification), and pliers (ETFs for efficiency). There are no contribution limits, but you pay taxes on any capital gains (profits from selling investments) realized within the account. Think of capital gains taxes as a fee you pay to use the toolbox. Taxable accounts are suitable for various investment goals, from long-term wealth building to holding assets you plan to sell in the short term. However, keep in mind the tax implications for short-term holdings.

Traditional IRAs (Individual Retirement Accounts): Your Tax-Advantaged Nest Egg Builder: These accounts offer significant tax advantages specifically for retirement savings. Contributions may be tax-deductible in the year you make them, like putting money into a tax-sheltered retirement account. Imagine Uncle Sam giving you a discount on your investment contributions! Your money then grows tax-deferred until you withdraw it in retirement. However, there are contribution limits and penalties for early withdrawals (before age 59 ½). Think of a traditional IRA as a specialized toolbox for retirement savings – it comes with tax benefits but also with restrictions on when you can access your money. Traditional IRAs are ideal for long-term retirement planning, especially if you're in a high tax bracket now and expect to be in a lower tax bracket in retirement. In that case, you'd be paying taxes on a potentially lower income in the future.

Roth IRAs: Your Tax-Free Wealth Generator: Similar to traditional IRAs, Roth IRAs offer tax benefits, but with a twist. Contributions are typically not tax-deductible, so you don't get an immediate tax break on the money you put in. However, your money grows tax-free, and qualified withdrawals in retirement are also tax-free. Imagine a Roth IRA as a special toolbox where your investments grow like magic, shielded from the taxman! This makes Roth IRAs a powerful tool for building tax-advantaged wealth for retirement. There are contribution limits, but unlike traditional IRAs, there are no penalties for early withdrawals of contributions (though earnings may still be subject to taxes and penalties). Roth IRAs are a great option for younger investors who have a long-time horizon and expect to be in a higher tax bracket in retirement. By using a Roth IRA, they can lock in today's potentially lower tax rates for their future withdrawals.

Choosing the Right Tools for the Job: Investment Strategies Tailored to Account Types

The optimal investment strategy for each account type depends on the tax implications and your investment goals. Here's a closer look at how to choose the right tools for each:

Taxable Brokerage Accounts: Prioritizing Long-Term Growth: Due to the taxation of capital gains, a long-term investment strategy is generally recommended for taxable accounts. Think of it like using your toolbox for a big renovation project, not a quick fix. Focus on a diversified portfolio of stocks, bonds, and other assets that can grow steadily over time. Consider using tax-efficient investment strategies like holding onto assets for more than a year to qualify for lower long-term capital gains tax rates. This is like maximizing the use of your tools without wasting money on unnecessary replacements.

Traditional IRAs: As you approach retirement, you may want to gradually shift your asset allocation towards a more conservative mix to preserve your capital. Think of this as transitioning your toolbox towards maintenance tools to ensure your retirement home remains in good shape. This strategy helps protect your accumulated savings from excessive risk as you near retirement.

Roth IRAs: Investing for Tax-Free Growth: Similar to traditional IRAs, a long-term investment strategy is recommended for Roth IRAs. However, since qualified withdrawals are tax-free, you have more flexibility in your investment choices. You can potentially invest in a wider range of assets within your Roth IRA toolbox, including growth-oriented stocks or even real estate investment trusts (REITs). Since your earnings grow tax-free, you can focus on maximizing your returns without worrying about tax implications. This allows you to build a substantial tax-free nest egg for retirement.

Building a Strong Foundation: Asset Allocation and Rebalancing

Choosing the right investment accounts is just the first step. Asset allocation refers to the strategy of dividing your investment portfolio across different asset classes like stocks, bonds, and cash equivalents. Imagine organizing your investment toolbox – stocks are your hammers for potential growth, bonds are your screwdrivers for stability, and cash equivalents are your spare nails for emergencies. There's no one-size-fits-all approach to asset allocation, but it typically considers your risk tolerance, investment goals, and time horizon. Younger investors with a longer time horizon may have a higher allocation towards stocks for potential growth, while those nearing retirement may prioritize bonds and cash equivalents for income and capital preservation.

Rebalancing is the process of periodically adjusting your asset allocation to maintain your desired risk profile. Over time, the market performance of different asset classes can cause your portfolio to drift away from your target allocation. Imagine your toolbox getting messy – some compartments might be overflowing with stocks (if the stock market has been doing well) while others might be depleted. Rebalancing involves buying or selling assets to ensure your toolbox remains organized and you have the right mix of tools for your investment goals. This helps you stay on track and manage risk effectively.

Investing is a journey, not a destination. Don't be tempted to chase fads or make impulsive decisions based on short-term market fluctuations. Develop a long-term investment plan, choose the right accounts and strategies for your goals, and stay disciplined. With knowledge, patience, and the right tools in your investment toolbox, you can build a secure and prosperous future. So, embark on your investment journey with confidence, and remember – a wise investor is a well-equipped investor!

CONCLUSION

We've explored the fundamentals of building a secure financial future, from creating a budget and saving consistently to conquering debt and harnessing the power of investing.

Remember, living within your means is the cornerstone of financial stability. Budgeting empowers you to allocate resources effectively and achieve your financial goals. Building an emergency fund and saving for the future are crucial aspects of financial security. Explore different savings vehicles and make saving a habit to watch your savings grow over time.

We tackled strategies for conquering debt, that relentless monster hindering financial freedom. You learned about prioritizing high-interest debt and different repayment methods like the debt avalanche or snowball approach. Remember, with dedication and a strategic plan, you can conquer debt and pave the way for a brighter financial future.

The exciting world of investing was unveiled as a powerful tool for wealth creation. We discussed choosing the right investment accounts based on your goals and time horizon, along with the importance of a diversified investment strategy and periodic rebalancing. Remember, investing is a marathon, so stay focused on your long-term plan and avoid impulsive decisions driven by market fluctuations.

We also emphasized investing in yourself, the most valuable asset you possess. Continuously develop your knowledge and skills to enhance your earning potential and explore ways to generate additional income streams. Remember, the more valuable you are in the marketplace, the greater your earning power and the faster you can achieve your financial goals.

Financial freedom is a journey, not a destination. Celebrate your milestones, big and small, and learn from setbacks. With dedication, perseverance, and the knowledge you've gained, you can unlock the door to financial freedom and build a secure and prosperous future.

So, take the first step today! Revisit your financial goals, refine your budget, and start implementing the strategies outlined here. Remember, the power to achieve financial freedom lies within you. With the right knowledge, tools, and mindset, you can transform your financial landscape and build a future filled with security, opportunity, and peace of mind. Go forth, empowered by financial knowledge, and embark on your journey toward a brighter financial future.

WHY **YOU** ARE STILL **BROKE!**